Wedding

INSPIRATION

Wedding

INSPIRATION

IDEAS & ADVICE *for* YOUR PERFECT WEDDING

KIMBERLY SCHLEGEL WHITMAN

with photography by DONNA NEWMAN

GIBBS SMITH
TO ENRICH AND INSPIRE HUMANKIND

First Edition

16 15 14 13 12   5 4 3 2 1

Text © 2012 Kimberly Schlegel Whitman
Photographs © 2012 Donna Newman

Published by
Gibbs Smith
P.O. Box 667
Layton, Utah 84041

1.800.835.4993 orders
www.gibbs-smith.com

Cover and book design by Michelle Farinella Design
Printed and bound in China
Gibbs Smith books are printed on either recycled, 100% post-consumer waste,
FSC-certified papers or on paper produced from sustainable PEFC-certified
forest/controlled wood source. Learn more at www.pefc.org.

Library of Congress Cataloging-in-Publication Data

Whitman, Kimberly Schlegel.
  Wedding inspiration : ideas & advice for your perfect wedding /
Kimberly Schlegel Whitman ; with photography by Donna Newman. — 1st ed.
    p. cm.
  ISBN 978-1-4236-2285-7
1. Weddings—Planning. I. Title.
  HQ745.W466 2012
  395.2'2—dc23
                    2012006744

For my mom, who is so inspiring

Contents

8

Acknowledgments

11

Introduction

Acknowledgments

There are so many wonderfully generous people I would like to acknowledge for their help with this book.

To Donna Newman, thank you for sharing your beautiful perspective and brides with us. Your kind smile and genuine warmth brings out the best in people and you have an extraordinary talent for capturing life's most precious celebrations.

To all of the brides who shared their journeys with me, I am so grateful. Thank you from the bottom of my heart for opening up the special moments in your life and helping new brides learn from your experiences.

I also want to acknowledge all of the wedding vendors whose work was featured in the book. Your hard work and brilliant ideas are creating magical memories for brides and grooms and their families and friends. Thank you for allowing me to share them in these pages.

To Madge, Hollie and the wonderful team at Gibbs Smith, Publisher, I am so grateful for the time, patience and attention to detail that you continue to put into my books. My gratitude for your belief in me can't be measured.

Thank you to my manager, Gladys Gonzalez, and my agent, Andrea Barzvi at ICM. Your wise council and advice are so appreciated and your loyalty and friendship means so much. Thank you to the amazing team at *Southern Living* and my fantastic radio family and the *Gene & Julie Show* and CBS Radio. I learn new things from all of you every day and I am so grateful for the opportunities you have provided for me.

To my family, thank you for supporting my passion for parties! I truly appreciate your patience and enthusiasm for my projects and your support means so much to me. I especially appreciate the love and efforts you all put into our family weddings. Dad, as you said in your toast at Kari and Troy's wedding, you believe that a marriage is very special and should be celebrated. That means so much to me.

I can't go with out mentioning my son who, at age three, was one of the best ring bearers I have ever seen. Your idea of ringing the bell as you walked down the aisle added magic to a very special day. I hope you continue to come up with new ideas and find great inspiration throughout your life.

To my husband, Justin, thank you for helping to make our marriage so beautiful. Our wedding was one of the most special days of my life but the marriage has been even more fun!

Introduction

As a little girl, I used to have sleepovers at my friend Summerlee's house, and we would go up to her room with scissors and bridal magazines and cut the ladies out and make wedding parties. We would pick a bride and then carefully select all the bridesmaids from the models photographed on the pages.

IT WAS SO MUCH FUN. We would stay up all night long putting on weddings with our special versions of paper dolls. Well, when we grew up and realized that weddings were more about marriage than fashion, we were not deterred. Summerlee was a bridesmaid in my wedding and I was honored be in her wedding too!

I think we all have stories like this from our childhood. You might not have gone so far as to carefully cut out magazines and stage your big day, but I bet you daydreamed a little bit! There is just something about that one special day that marks an amazing commitment. Once we pick our grooms, we want to successfully celebrate with style, fun and joy.

For some people, inspiration comes easily. Their vision for their big day has been as clear as a bell since their grade-school slumber parties. For others, finding meaningful inspiration can be like pulling teeth—painful! Pulling together a vision for a celebration can be hard and stressful, but I believe that, with a clear idea of your inspiration, your big day will be one of dreams fulfilled.

Thank you for letting me be a part of your plans for your wedding. I hope this book will help you either find your inspirations for your special day or narrow down the focus of the inspirations you have held dear for many years.

Finding Your Inspiration

Creating an inspiration board is the first thing you should do after you become engaged. Your board will help you discover the look and mood you want to set for your big day, but it will also help you communicate it to wedding vendors and make important commitments and arrangements.

Finding your true wedding style is one thing but communicating it to your vendors is another! That is why I love the process of putting together an inspiration board. Your board could be made from a piece of poster board from a craft store, a box that holds swatches, ideas and fabrics, or it could be a digital image or PowerPoint presentation. I don't think it matters what form it is in. It only matters that you piece together the ideas and items that inspire you so that you can visualize your wedding mood, theme and look.

The First Steps

✦

THE FIRST STEP to finding your wedding inspiration is to ask yourself a few questions. You might have a clear and concise answer to each one or you may find this to be a really challenging exercise. Either way, carefully think through your answers, discuss them with your groom and your family, and record your thoughts. Your answers are important because you will refer to them as you make decisions regarding every element of your big day, from the invitations to the parting favors.

What adjectives first come to mind when you describe your groom's personality?

What adjectives first come to mind when you describe your own personality?

What elements of your history or family heritage do you want to honor on your special day?

Describe the best party you have ever attended.

Describe the most fun dates you and your future spouse have been on.

Describe the most beautiful wedding you have ever attended.

What is your personal style?

If you could decorate your home any way you would like, what would it look like?

What is your favorite place on Earth? Describe it in three words. Maybe it is a beach, the mountains or a country village? Maybe it is a modernist house, a museum or a bench in a park.

Using the answers to the questions above, select three adjectives you want your guests to use when describing your wedding to their friends and family in the days after the celebration.

Here are some suggested words that I hope will spark some thoughtful answers:

Architectural	Hip
Avant-garde	Historical
Charming	Informal
Chic	Irreverent
Classic	Minimalist
Clean	Modern
Creative	Over the Top
Decadent	Playful
Dreamy	Romantic
Elegant	Royal
Emotional	Serious
Ethereal	Sophisticated
Fancy	Sweet
Fashionable	Touching
Festive	Traditional
Formal	Understated
Fun	Unique
Glamorous	

Now that you have three words you can use to describe your wedding, you can start assembling your inspiration board. Simply select the item you want to use to make your board. I suggest a solid poster board available from any craft store. Purchase a white or neutral board, even if you find one in the color you want to use for your wedding. You will cover it in your words, inspirational photos, mementos and materials. Next, write the three descriptive words at the top of the board, either in your own handwriting or in your favorite computerized font.

Now you are ready to start attaching images and items that have meaning to you. Go ahead and attach things that might not fit the three words you selected if they are special to you. Your wedding vendors might be able to find a way to make those things fit in and work. The items could be anything from a paint chip of a color that you know you want to incorporate, a ribbon from a bouquet of flowers that your groom sent to you, a photo from a favorite vacation, a fashion spread pulled from a magazine, or ideas you have pulled from bridal magazines. Whatever you have that inspires you should be included!

After you have put it all on the board, stand back with your groom or your bridesmaids and really think about what you have there. How does everything fit together? How are all of the items similar? What do they all have in common? Once you have tied them together, you have uncovered your underlying theme. Congratulations! You have just unlocked the key to keeping your wedding stylish and cohesive!

Use the inspiration board and its similarities to help you make all your decisions moving forward. If you are stuck between two dresses and can't make up your mind, ask yourself which one best fits with your inspiration board. If you have spent hours flipping through the big invitation books at your favorite stationery stores, take your board in with you and ask the professionals if they have something that fits your theme.

Your inspiration board is the trick to making wedding planning simple. You have a guide to help make every single overwhelming decision. It is like having a stylish fairy godmother peeking over your shoulder asking you how your decisions fit in!

The Wedding of

Stephanie and Eric

April 2, 2011

FROM EVERY HUMAN BEING THERE RISES A LIGHT THAT REACHES
STRAIGHT TO HEAVEN. AND WHEN TWO SOULS THAT ARE DESTINED TO
BE TOGETHER FIND EACH OTHER, THEIR STREAMS OF LIGHT FLOW TOGETHER,
AND A SINGLE BRIGHTER LIGHT GOES FORTH FROM THEIR UNITED BEING.

Kabbalah

Expert Opinions

❧

THE INVITATIONS

"Select invitations that complement the overall design of your wedding. Follow etiquette when doing your wording."

—Mary Wright-Shah, wedding planner

"Your wedding invitations will set the tone for your celebration. Small details will make a huge impact that will impress the recipient and create excitement for your wedding."

—Nick and Aleah Valley, wedding and event planners and designers, Valley & Co.

"I love hand-done calligraphy. It is so amazing and adds so much to the overall feeling of an invitation."

—Jon Buick, event planner and designer for Xquisite Events

"The invitation will visually represent your personal style and let your guests know the level of formality for your nuptials. I like to see the invites coordinate with the colors you have chosen for your wedding and all printed items stay with the same design, font and paper. Create a sense of continuity by designing all your printed materials the same."

—Susan Spindler, event and wedding coordinator and designer

"The invitation is the true preview to the wedding day so it should reflect the mood and style the guests will find when they arrive."

—Laurie Arons, wedding planner and designer

"Gorgeous and luscious calligraphy on a simple cardstock or linen paper is always apropos."

—James T. Farmer, III, lifestyle expert and editor-at-large for *Southern Living*

"The invitation is the calling card for your event. This is a place for you to incorporate your wedding colors, logo and style—making it a representation of you. Whether you are sending a save the date photo or a custom box filled with items from your exotic wedding destination, this is the area to get your guests excited for your upcoming wedding."

—Katherine Mathes and Emily Rembert, event planners, Mathes and Co.

"There is a saying that you only get one chance to make a first impression. We believe your invitation is that first impression and can become the 'common thread' found in every key element of your wedding—whether it's an image of a palm tree, your monogram, or colors and visual details—and it should continue until the last guest leaves."

—Cheryl Beitler and Dale Flam, event and wedding planners for The Zanadu Group

"The invitation is the very first detail that sets the tone for the wedding and gives guests a taste of what's to come! Invitations have come a long way since the days of black ink engraved on solid card stocks, and brides have tons of options. Choose what you love! My biggest tip is to stay consistent with all printed materials, from the invitations to the menu cards to the favor tags. This will give the event a beautifully cohesive impression from start to finish."

—Camille Styles, event planner and editor of CamilleStyles.com

The Gown

"Don't be afraid to try on different styles. The one that you've always thought would be 'perfect' may not be as flattering as you thought. You'll know it the moment you look at yourself in the mirror."

—Cheryl Beitler and Dale Flam, event and wedding planners for The Zanadu Group

"Don't go strapless!"

—Tara Guérard, event designer and owner of Tara Guérard Soiree

"Finding a frame and style that suits your body type is the most important part of finding the dress. Once you've found the right fit, you can continue your search for stunning designs and detailing like beading and sashes."

—Nick and Aleah Valley, wedding and event planners and designers, Valley & Co.

"First select the date and venue, then it's time to start shopping for the gown. Ultimately, brides should pick the gown they feel most beautiful in—if you find yourself smiling in one more than any other, that is probably the one for you."

—Laurie Arons, wedding planner and designer

"If you aren't used to wearing five-inch heels, don't pick this day to do so."

—Susan Spindler, event and wedding coordinator and designer

"Make sure it's completely comfortable. No matter how beautiful the dress, you won't enjoy wearing it if you're having to tug or pull at it all night."

—Camille Styles, event planner and editor of CamilleStyles.com

"Take the classicism of yesteryear and add a modern touch. Embrace your physique!"

—James T. Farmer, III, lifestyle expert and editor-at-large for Southern Living

"Pick what makes you feel confident, beautiful and yourself."

—Mary Wright-Shah, wedding planner

The Cake

"The cake is the perfect sweet ending to your special day."

—Katherine Mathes and Emily Rembert, event planners, Mathes and Co.

"Many couples are considering individual cakes for each guest!"

—Susan Spindler, event and wedding coordinator and designer

"Whatever you design, don't be afraid to be a little daring and make a statement with your wedding cake."

—Nick and Aleah Valley, wedding and event planners and designers, Valley & Co.

"A cake tasting is key. Taste the flavors while looking through portfolios to see what styles they offer."

—Laurie Arons, wedding planner and designer

"No matter how beautiful your cake is, make sure it tastes amazing! That is one of the first questions I get about a wedding, how did the cake taste?"

—Mary Wright-Shah, wedding planner

"The cake should be the grand finale at the end of an unforgettable day!"

—Camille Styles, event planner and editor of CamilleStyles.com

"It MUST be delicious! Wedding cakes have grown and grown and can lose flavor that way. A simple but DELICIOUS cake makes for a more memorable confection. To feed the masses, have your cake maker make petit fours or cupcakes from the batter of the bride's cake so everyone can enjoy a fabulous confection."

—James T. Farmer, III, lifestyle expert and editor-at-large for *Southern Living*

"*We like to showcase the wedding cake so your guests will be able to see it before the cake cutting and can appreciate the thought that went into its design. Let them also be amazed when it even tastes as good as it looks!*"

—Cheryl Beitler and Dale Flam, event and wedding planners for
The Zanadu Group

"*Make it a mix of all your ideas . . . don't copy an exact design from anyone else!*"

—Tara Guérard, event designer and owner of Tara Guérard Soiree

THE VENUE

"The venue is an important decision as it sets the tone for all other aspects of the wedding. Of course you want to select a place that is beautiful and fits your vision. The more a venue offers in terms of atmosphere, the less you will have to do with flowers and décor."

—Laurie Arons, wedding planner and designer

"There are three criteria that you should consider when selecting the venue—budget, capacity and location."

—Katherine Mathes and Emily Rembert, event planners, Mathes and Co.

"Search for a venue that represents your style, one that allows for a comfortable wedding, can accommodate your guests and, most importantly, one that is special to you."

—Nick and Aleah Valley, wedding and event planners and designers, Valley & Co.

"Location. Location. Location. The venue you select will make a statement the moment your guests read it on your invitation. It speaks to how you define romance and the lifestyle that you envision for yourselves. It says casual, beach chic or baroque opulence. It speaks of your vision for the perfect once-in-a-lifetime event."

—Cheryl Beitler and Dale Flam, event and wedding planners for The Zanadu Group

"Choose the right venue for the size of your guest list. Nothing kills a party faster than feeling like a room is empty because the space is way too big for the group. If you're working with a smaller guest list, choose a venue that feels intimate. If it's a huge party, make sure there is ample space with lots of smaller conversation areas so guests can sit and talk away from the dance floor."

—Camille Styles, event planner and editor of CamilleStyles.com

"Choose a venue that matches the time of your event."

—Mary Wright-Shah, wedding planner

"With each venue there are different things to consider: When can you set up? What time do you need to be out? What are the kitchen facilities like? Will you need rentals? The reception and food will be the largest part of your budget so determining the number of guests can play a part in your venue selection."

—Susan Spindler, event and wedding coordinator and designer

"If you can tent, then tent! There is nothing more quintessential than a white tent and twinkling lights. That's not always an option, so use bunting, lighting, garland, etc., to make a tent effect in a ballroom or wherever you might be."

—James T. Farmer, III, lifestyle expert and editor-at-large for *Southern Living*

ENTERTAINMENT

"Think outside the box to make it a true reflection of the bride and groom! I've booked entertainment from a string quartet to a mariachi band to a faux tattoo artist and all were equally perfect for the unique couple I was working with. Music totally sets the mood, so make the decision based on how you define "fun!"

—Camille Styles, event planner and editor of CamilleStyles.com

"What's on your iPod Shuffle? Have that band play!"

—James T. Farmer, III, lifestyle expert and editor-at-large for *Southern Living*

"Get several referrals."

—Tara Guérard, event designer and owner of Tara Guérard Soiree

"Keep in mind when picking out music that each chapter of the wedding day has its own energy and mood. Pick your music accordingly."

—Susan Spindler, event and wedding coordinator and designer

"If people are the heart of an event, the entertainment is its soul. If you know the genre and vibe that you want to create for your guests, both heart and soul will be merged to create the perfect sensory experience."

—Cheryl Beitler and Dale Flam, event and wedding planners for The Zanadu Group

"Whatever you want to incorporate, be sure to see the entertainment or band in person. Remember that your guests will be entertained by the unexpected."

—Nick and Aleah Valley, wedding and event planners and designers, Valley & Co.

"Choose wisely. This choice can really make or break your night. Choose entertainment that is versatile and can accommodate a mixed audience."

—Mary Wright-Shah, wedding planner

INSPIRATION

"A bride brought me a piece of torn lace from her grandmother's gown. She had a photo of her grandparents' big day, complete with flowers. We had her dress re-created from that patch of old lace and updated the flowers too, but the presence of her grandparents, who had recently passed, was there the whole day . . . from the lace to the flowers, it was all truly delightful."

—James T. Farmer, III, lifestyle expert and editor-at-large for Southern Living

"After a groom proposed with crystals on the bottom of a pair of shoes, they became our Cinderella and Prince Charming and we their Fairy God Planners."

—Cheryl Beitler and Dale Flam, event and wedding planners for The Zanadu Group

"The most unusual item a bride has brought to me for wedding inspiration was a Tony Duquette book (by Hutton Wilkinson) . . . WOW! Filled with unique ideas and I loved it!"

—Tara Guérard, event designer and owner of Tara Guérard Soiree

EXPERT OPINIONS

"Always remember a party is a reflection of you so be true to yourself, your feelings and your budget. Explore all possibilities so that, in the end, it was part of you and no one else."

—Jon Buick, event planner and designer for Xquisite Events

"A couple brought us old Victorian cake pulls she found in her hometown of New Orleans. The tradition of cake pulls was new to us but it inspired much of their wedding vision. We tied in other Victorian traditions and New Orleans flair. From a muted Mardi Gras palette to use of the fleur-de-lis in the stationery and a ceremonial cake pull, this wonderful tradition laid the blueprint for a celebration rich in history, tradition and flair."

—Nick and Aleah Valley, wedding and event planners and designers, Valley & Co.

"We had a bride and groom who were engaged at a venue that was very special to them. They brought us the logo of the venue and we designed a wedding logo around it, making it personal and unique to the couple."

—Katherine Mathes and Emily Rembert, event planners, Mathes and Co.

"A bride brought me an Indonesian-inspired elephant she found engraved on a piece of stationery. She loved the vibrant colors and the intricate detail she wanted in her celebration."

—Mary Wright-Shah, wedding planner

"One couple I recently worked with wanted to honor the groom's father, who had recently passed away, by having the groom don his dad's French blue silk tie for the ceremony. It was such a gorgeous color, we decided to use that tie as the inspiration for the entire event, creating a beautiful vision in French blue, ivory and champagne."

—Camille Styles, event planner and editor of CamilleStyles.com

Beautiful Weddings

Kari Schlegel & Troy Kloewer

When my sister, Kari, came back from a beach walk with her boyfriend, Troy, at our lake house with a ring on her finger, I was jumping with joy! Not only because I was happy for her, but also because I was thrilled that I could get back to planning a family wedding! I had been married for five years and I was ready to run with this!

Troy was a friend of my brother and my husband and, when he started dating Kari, the boys were thrilled! They loved the idea of having this nice, hardworking, fun guy around the family. The girls were thrilled because we loved seeing Kari so happy! They were a natural fit from the start and their engagement was truly celebrated.

Kari had a few ideas about what she wanted for her wedding but she had very few specifics in mind. She knew she wanted her guests to say WOW, she wanted it to feel intimate in spite of the large guest list, and she knew she wanted all-white flowers. My mother, Kari and I sat down with a few members of her wedding team to bring her inspirations to life.

THE GOWN

The details started to come together as she tried on wedding dresses. She had a gown made by Monique Lhuillier in Los Angeles and based many of the details of the wedding on the design of the gown. Her choice was a strapless A-line gown in white lace that was covered in a layer of tulle with gorgeous floral beading on top. The result was a feminine combination of traditional lace and modern tulle that sparked the look for the rest of the wedding. The tricky part of the gown was that it was being custom made and she was not able to try it on until a few weeks before the wedding. We knew what it would look like from the sketches and fabric swatches, but we didn't really know exactly what the end result would be. It ended up being even more spectacular than we ever dreamed. Her train was ten feet long and was covered in ethereal tulle. After the ceremony, the lace train was removed and the long tulle layer was bustled into a gorgeous cloud-like skirt on the back of her dress. It was so pretty and matched the rest of the wedding, from the mood to the tablecloths, to perfection.

THE INVITATIONS

The details of the wedding started to come together after the dress was designed. It became the leader of the inspiration board. When put into words, the wedding was shaping up to be traditional with a veil of modern, feminine and sparkly. When it was time to select the invitations, an engraved invitation from The Printery in silver ink on a heavy ply card was written out in calligraphy. It was traditional in every way, including the personalization that we added, but it was presented with a dramatic modern flare. At the top of each invitation, a line was left open so that a calligrapher could write in the names of the guests on each personalized invitation. The modern twist came into play with a lovely silver box that was created by Paradise Design Co. to deliver the invitation and its accessories. A reply card and the invitations to the rest of the weekend's festivities were put behind a ribbon at the back of the box. The traditional invitation was placed on top so that it was the first thing the guests spotted when they opened the box.

As the replies started to arrive, the tent was designed. It was set up across the street from the church so that the guests could simply exit the ceremony and walk across the street for the reception.

The Wedding Party

The bridesmaids came down the aisle one by one in silver gowns designed by the bride and Dallas couturier Michael Faircloth. Kari took her inspirations, including an image of a pink strapless gown with beading at the top, to her first meeting with Michael and he drew some sketches to help capture on paper what the two had dreamed up. Kari also liked the idea of having an embellished knot and more decoration on the back of the dresses as that is the part of the gown that most of the guests had a view of during the ceremony. The results were glamorous and met Kari's criteria for a mix of modern and traditional.

After the twelve bridesmaids made their way down the aisle, an emotional trip for me, the junior bridesmaids started down. Troy's nieces and Kari's cousin were in dresses made from the same deep silver satin, but they had a more age-appropriate cut. They had tulle tops that covered their chests and A-line skirts. My son, JR, who served as the ring bearer, followed them. He mentioned, months before the wedding, that he would prefer to ring a bell at the wedding instead of carrying a box or pillow, so, in a break with tradition, he dramatically announced the arrival of the bride and our father by ringing a monogrammed bell with all of his might as he marched down the aisle with a smile. The honor attendants, dressed in pretty gray dresses from J. Crew's bridal collection, were seated and ready to arrange Kari's train as she settled at the altar.

After Kari was led down the aisle by our father, they were met by her groom, their wedding party and Rev. Mark Craig at the altar. Kari had chosen to cover the altar table in the same cloth that Justin and I had at our wedding. It was made from a piece of antique textile that we purchased at a flea market on a trip to Paris. Kari and Troy also chose to take communion on the same antique kneelers that Justin and I had

at our wedding. It meant so much to us to see their choice. I hope our unmarried brother and sister will carry on the tradition at their future wedding ceremonies!

Rev. Craig shared touching words with the congregation about marriage and relationships. He shared fun family stories and the personal touches made his words meaningful and memorable. I fought back tears for most of the ceremony!

Everyone who knows Kari knows that she is a self-proclaimed princess. She loves pink, glamour and getting dressed up. When it came time to design her bouquet, the amazing event designer, Todd Fiscus of todd.event design.creative, took her inspirations, requests and her personality into play. He went with a royal-style cascading bouquet of orchids. It was all white and the orchids seemed to simply fall from her hands. It was also a perfect complement to her dress.

KARI SCHLEGEL & TROY KLOEWER

THE RECEPTION

The reception was held in a tent across the street from the church. It was so nice to be able to simply walk across the street and be at the party instead of driving to a second location. A soft gray carpet was laid out across the street for the guests to walk on. Although a few cars had to pass over it, it stayed fairly clean and was a wonderful guide to get the guests to the reception.

The guests were greeted in a small cupola tent with clear panels. A round table with a beautiful white floral arrangement was placed in the center of the room with the escort cards laid out alphabetically.

The seated dinner took place in a grand tent. The décor was dramatic, glamorous and the perfect blend of traditional and modern. It looked much like a white and silver version of Kari's home!

As the doors were opened to the dinner tent, the couple's amazing wedding cake was front and center. It was an incredible seven feet tall and very dramatic. The all-white cake was covered in orange blossom sugar flowers and certainly got the "wow" factor that Kari had requested.

Following the delicious meal that highlighted cuisine that was in peak season, the guests were invited to gather on the dance floor by a charming little cheesecake ball with a message flag attached. They were delivered to each seat and enjoyed immediately!

After a fun-filled night of toasts, dancing, mingling and dining, the guests picked up amazing dogwood branches made out of silver with a gift tag that read: love blooms.

Although Kari says she wishes that her wedding day could have lasted forever, she looks back on it with fond memories. The planning process, from finding her inspiration to carrying out the big plans, was so much fun and I will always cherish the fun times we had together during the process.

KARI SCHLEGEL & TROY KLOEWER

KARI SCHLEGEL & TROY KLOEWER

Please join us
for cake
and dancing!

Be Inspired

✦ Your inspiration can come from anywhere! Consider tearing photographs from interior design or fashion magazines to add to your inspiration boards.

✦ Don't veer far away from your everyday style. Embrace your own everyday look but kick it up a notch for your wedding day.

✦ Remember that the back of your bridesmaid's dresses is as important as the front. Your guests will be looking at the back of them throughout the ceremony, so consider adding a detail to the back of their gowns or their hair.

✦ Have ideas for what you want but be open-minded. Kari's wedding designer, Todd, had to talk her into a cascading bouquet, but it ended up being the perfect touch!

✦ Ask your family members and friends about their own wedding celebrations and incorporate elements from their ceremonies into yours. We were honored when Kari and Troy asked us if they could use our altar cloth. Hopefully my other family members will use it too!

✦ Kari's Advice for Future Brides: "Just go with the flow! Don't stress because what's done is done and the most important thing is that you have fun."

Lucky Tradition

Something Old: The altar cloth used in Kari and Troy's wedding was purchased at a flea market in Paris and used in my wedding to Justin five years ago.

Something New: Kari received a gift of diamond earrings from our parents.

Something Borrowed: Kari borrowed our mother's necklace to enhance her strapless dress.

Something Blue: The insides of Kari's shoes were blue!

Kari Schlegel & Troy Kloewer

Alexandra Alder & Michael Toccin

When fashion is the focus of both the bride and grooms careers, it is no surprise that a proposal happened appropriately at Neiman Marcus over a pair of red soles!

Michael and Alexandra met at Georgetown University orientation and ended up living across the hall from each other in the co-ed dorms. The relationship grew and they developed a passion for fashion that took them to New York City together. After stints at Parsons, they both have dream careers in high fashion.

After his proposal in perfect fashion, the couple set out to plan a wedding inspired by their passion. Both Alex and Michael are from Florida so the Ritz Carlton Grand Lakes in Orlando seemed like the perfect location. The guest list was set at 280 and the couple started making plans together.

The Gown

Michael's work in fashion made his opinion very valuable, so Alex and Michael, along with Alex's mother, made every decision together. That is, with one exception, Alex's gown. She wanted that to be a surprise. After trying on gowns from a variety of designers, Alex chose a beautiful silhouette from Vera Wang. The gorgeous gown flattered her figure and was the perfect inspiration for the cake, which took its shape and details from the gown. Alex's choice was a clear winner with Michael, who smiled from ear to ear when he saw her before the ceremony.

The cake was not the only thing inspired by the gown. The lace on the tablecloths matched the lace on the dress as well. Alex's attention to detail made the wedding come together with a cohesive and elegant look that was carried through, from the welcome bag for the out-of-towners to the chair covers at the reception.

The Invitations

The couple loved working with Ceci Johnson of Ceci New York on the invitations because she made the process so easy. She took their love of the 1940s and mixed it with a modern and traditional theme. The look for the paper goods was carried through the entire weekend of events, from the invitation and welcome package to the menu and escort cards. The gold and ivory color scheme was carried throughout in every detail.

The Flowers

Flowers and fashion are an easy mix, so Michael Ereshena of The Special Event Resource and Design Group managed to include almost every type of flower imaginable! Alex requested hydrangea and peonies but didn't realize the extent

of her options until she went flower picking in New York with her talented floral designer. Their early morning jaunt took place two weeks before the wedding and Alex loved everything she saw!

The final results did not disappoint! Alex's bouquet was full of gorgeous white flowers with various textures and sizes. The details on the bouquet echoed her gorgeous gown and had flair to match. All the textures and styles from the couples shared love of fashion were evident throughout the celebration and they all came together with style.

Personal touches were everywhere. Alex incorporated family into her bouquet by carrying a locket from her grandmother and a necklace from Michael's great grandmother in her tussy mussy. The welcome baskets for the guests included the couple's favorite things, from a chocolate-covered shoe to Pop Chips.

Alex's favorite memory of the day was the few moments that the new husband and wife spent alone in the ballroom before the guests entered. They took some time to take it all in as Mr. and Mrs. Michael Toccin. The gorgeous room inspired an intimate dance and the moment is one they will never forget.

THE CEREMONY

A semester shared in Florence also influenced the couple's wedding look. The ceremony décor was inspired by an Italian garden, and the view from the end of the aisle resembled the gorgeous design of Italy's most elaborate landscapes. The green garlands and white flowers framed the couple in a beautiful chuppah. The traditional Jewish ceremony was intimate and grand, modern and traditional, and captured the Italian beauty that the couple was inspired by during their semester abroad.

Mr. and Mrs. Jeffrey Alan Adler
request the honour of your presence
at the marriage of their daughter

Alexandra Rochelle

to

Mr. Michael David Toccin

Saturday, the twenty-sixth of March
Two thousand and eleven
at half past seven o'clock

The Ritz-Carlton Orlando, Grande Lakes
Orlando, Florida

Dinner and Dancing to

ALEXANDRA ALDER & MICHAEL TOCCIN

THE RECEPTION

After the Italian garden–themed ceremony and the traditional and fashion-oriented dinner, a 1940's nightclub-themed after party ensued. The lounge area had a more modern feeling to it but celebrated a glamorous era that this couple admired. The mirrored bar set the area apart and the waiters in black tie served the couple's favorite snacks—quesadillas, grilled cheese sandwiches and chocolate-covered strawberries.

Their nickname for each other was the name of the late-night dessert station they set up as Pop's Bakery. Fashion-inspired cupcakes with edible glitz and sequin details were set out for the guests to enjoy later. As a sweet ending to a scrumptious day, to-go boxes were provided so that guests could make their bakery selections and fill their own boxes.

An amazing amount of detailed attention went into planning the celebration of Alex and Michael's marriage. Their vision of a fashion-filled, forties theme with Italian touches was brought together through an elegant color scheme and personal touches.

ALEXANDRA ALDER & MICHAEL TOCCIN

+ Celebrate what you love. Alex and Michael love fashion, so they incorporated it into every facet of their special day.

+ Include meaningful symbols. Michael proposed over a pair of shoes, so the clever couple gave chocolate shoes to each guest to enjoy.

+ Personalize it! There are so many wonderful ways to include personal touches. Alex and Michael incorporated their nickname for each other, Pops, into the late-night sweets by creating Pop's Bakery.

+ Plan to have a few minutes alone. Alex and Michael planned a sweet escape into the ballroom for a few minutes before the guests were invited in so that they could soak it all up!

+ Alex's Advice for Future Brides: "It is so important to have a fantastic photographer and videographer to capture the day because it goes by so quickly. We watch our wedding video once or twice a week!"

Lucky Tradition

Something Old: Alex carried her grandmother's locket and a necklace from Michael's grandmother with her bouquet.

Something New: Alex's parents gave her a beautiful diamond bracelet that she wore on her big day, which echoed the elegant 1940's theme of the wedding.

Something Borrowed: Alex borrowed her future mother-in-law's diamond-and-pearl earrings.

Something Blue: Of course, after becoming engaged over a pair of Christian Louboutin shoes, Alex had to wear red soles on her big day, but the kicker was the I DO crystal embellishment that peeked out in blue.

ALEXANDRA ALDER & MICHAEL TOCCIN

Carolyn Rubenstein & Ben Spoont

When a Harvard PhD candidate who runs a charitable foundation is planning a wedding, she turns to mom for lots of help. Carolyn Rubenstein met her future husband, Ben Spoont, in high school calculus. Although it wasn't the most romantic setting, he made up for it with an intimate proposal at a private mountain picnic near Twin Farms in Vermont. The bride was into scrapbooking, so the groom got to work creating a scrapbook about their relationship. The final page held the ring so, of course, the bride said yes!

They immediately set out for a planned trip to Paris and Rome with Carolyn's family. The trip was a great celebration and source of inspiration for the bride and her mother. The bride-to-be returned to Boston and made plans during trips home and by phone with her mother. She selected Mar-a-Lago, Marjorie Merriwether Post's incredible Palm Beach, Florida, estate, as the location. Mar-a-Lago is now a private club established by Donald Trump. Mr. Trump and his wife, Melania, built an amazing ballroom on the grounds of the estate in time for their own magnificent wedding. The bride's parents are members of the club, so it was a perfect fit for the glorious celebration.

The talented Michael Ereshena of The Special Event Resource & Design Group was hired to produce the wedding décor. The bride requested a neutral palette to complement the amazing ballroom, but she also gave Michael a photo from a wedding that was on *The Today Show*. Carolyn loved the photograph because "everything glowed!" She asked Michael to capture that glow for her special day. The flashes of pink in the neutral bouquets inspired her and she knew she wanted to have that same glow in the room on her wedding day.

Carolyn also knew that she wanted a traditional wedding that felt like a magical fairy tale. The creams and golds of the ballroom were her main color scheme, but her inspiration came from *The Today Show* wedding image, and the flashes of color she adored came alive in the neutral background.

THE GOWN

Carolyn and her mother met in New York for a weekend of dress shopping, and her first two appointments left her feeling discouraged. She had an image in her mind of what she was looking for. She thought she wanted a classic full skirt in lace and a bodice with cap sleeves. Her only concern was that a big white gown might overpower her petite frame. After a few appointments with no luck, she ended up at Bergdorf's, where her mother asked her to try on a gown that was exactly what she knew she did not want! Her mother coaxed her into trying on a Carolina Herrera gown covered in sweet little flowers. Once Carolyn had it on, she realized that this was the one. So many brides talk about "just knowing" when it comes to both the groom and the dress!

THE INVITATIONS

Carolyn's inspiration also came from classic royal weddings, especially that of Princess Grace of Monaco. The elegant wedding invitations she chose could certainly have come by royal proclamation! The classic Cartier cards were cream with a gold beveled

border and gold script. The style was carried through, from the save-the-date announcements to the menu cards. They were elegant in their simplicity but magical in their fairy-tale wedding opulence.

THE WEDDING PARTY

Carolyn's seven bridesmaids included her sister as her maid of honor. Carolina Herrera's designs included an evening gown with the same floral design as the wedding gown Carolyn had selected, so her sister dazzled in the coordinating gown in slate gray. The rest of the wedding party wore black one-shoulder gowns by Alvina Valenta that Carolyn selected for their small details, such as a bow on the shoulders and a small train in the back.

THE CEREMONY

Carolyn described the moments before the ceremony, when it was just her and her mother alone in the bride's room at Mar-a-Lago, as her favorite memory of the big day. It was the calm before things got started and she cherished the special private time they had together. The same rabbi who married Carolyn's parents and presided over her baby naming and bat mitzvah led the traditional Jewish

ceremony. This personal touch added a traditional element to the ceremony even though Carolyn thought outside the box in a number of ways as well. She left out some traditions and added in others, which held special meaning for the couple and their families. Carolyn opted not to circle the groom seven times, because she wanted to start their marriage off on equal ground, but the couple did sign the ketubah in front of the guests instead of in a private ceremony before the wedding. Carolyn said, "Signing the ketubah during the ceremony only added a few minutes to the length of the ceremony and it was really special to have so many special witnesses." She also insisted that she didn't want Ben to see her before the ceremony, so they avoided the separate ketubah ceremony.

CAROLYN RUBENSTEIN & BEN SPOONT

THE RECEPTION

The seated dinner was set up on long rectangular tables. The main table was the largest and was set up in the center of the room. To warm up the enormous ballroom a bit, Carolyn's mother had extra chandeliers brought in and hung at a lower level than the existing ones. It certainly did the trick and made a dramatic statement at the same time.

CAROLYN RUBENSTEIN & BEN SPOONT

CAROLYN RUBENSTEIN & BEN SPOONT

Nina Johnson & Daniel Milewski

Until you see the parking garage at 1111 Lincoln Road in Miami, you might balk at the idea of a wedding in a parking space. Eleven Eleven was developed as a multi-use space that doubled as both a parking garage and an event space. Sounds like an odd combination, but when Gallery Diet owner Nina Johnson and artist Daniel Milewski saw the space, they knew it was exactly what they wanted for

their wedding celebration. The ceilings were thirty feet high and the views from the seventh floor were spectacular. The space was carefully planned during development and included strategically placed electrical outlets. The bumps and grooves that marked the parking spaces were easily removed to create the perfect event venue.

Nina and Daniel met when Nina's gallery represented his work. In their six years together, the couple's strong bond helped them developed a sense of what they wanted for their big day. Daniel loves to get dressed up, so they knew they wanted a black-tie event. He is typically in studio clothes, so marking a special occasion means donning special duds! They also felt that guests at the wedding were certainly part of the décor. The black-tie attire would certainly add refinement to a rough space.

Eleven Eleven also proved to be the perfect spot for Nina and Daniel to celebrate their marriage because, as Nina put it, "it let the support systems show." The structure's interesting architecture allowed for each beam and support to remain exposed and play a role in the design. The architecture was a huge inspiration for the bride and groom, a natural fit for two aesthetic people. They ended up embracing the idea of a "garden party in the sky!"

The leftover construction materials from the new parking garage enhanced the atmosphere in the space. The architects of Eleven Eleven made furniture for the wedding out of the boards that were used to make the building!

THE GOWN

Nina didn't want a traditional gown but she did want details. She found a gorgeous gown by Oscar de la Renta. She knew it was "the gown" but wanted a little something more as well. When she saw the runway images of a coordinating bolero jacket, she knew she had to have it. After receiving the discouraging news that the jacket was not ever produced and was created only for the runway, she pleaded and ended up wearing the sample piece!

THE INVITATIONS

Standard invitations would not do for these art lovers. The bride and groom wanted something unique so they turned to artist Abby Manock who created a silhouette of the building and an image with the bear and butterfly. Abby's creation was sent to Mr. Boddington's Studio. The studio created an invitation

suite that included a small card describing the black-tie attire that was requested in full Victorian language.

The art of the stationery didn't stop with the invitations. Limited edition artist's prints of Abby's work were created as the party favors for the wedding guests but ended up being sent out with the thank-you cards instead.

THE WEDDING PARTY

Nina asked her wedding party to make their own dress selections. Her two adult bridesmaids and two junior bridesmaids selected their own black dresses to suit their taste and figures. Nina commissioned Nektar de Stagni to create earrings for the wedding party out of pearls and black diamonds. Don't worry, the groomsmen were not left out. Daniel gave each member of his wedding party an antique pocket watch to commemorate the special time.

THE CEREMONY

The ceremony was magical but windy! When Nina got the call from her event coordinators at Fiction Events in the hours before the wedding that the red flowers and candles they had made arrangements for would not stay down in the heavy winds blowing through the garage, she didn't fret. Instead, she called Daniel who assured her that everything would be wonderful. He advised her not think about what they can't change and just be happy for what they have. Brilliant advice for every bride!

When the time came, a talented gospel singer sang "If I Needed You" as Nina came down the aisle without a bouquet. Instead she wanted her hands to be in her pockets. A stylish look that suited the high-fashion runway-ready gown she had selected.

NINA JOHNSON & DANIEL MILEWSKI

THE RECEPTION

To accommodate their 200 guests, two long tables holding 100 guests each were laid down the center of the space. They were covered in burlap cloths and LED candles. The plan was to cover the tables in arrangements of red roses as well, but that was canceled because of the winds. The simple design added drama to the already fabulous space.

Many of the guests took a moment to run down to the first floor of the parking structure, where the retail shops sold hats, scarves and mittens to the guests who were chillier than expected on floor seven! It was an unexpected chill but proved to be a fun element to the party!

Daniel's father, a musician, played and sang the first dance for the couple. The dance proved to be Nina's favorite memory of the wedding day. It seemed like a quiet moment that was just about the new Mr. and Mrs.

The menu was all about family-style comfort food. Mac and cheese and other home-style family favorites were passed down the two long tables, and the coffee stand proved a popular spot in fighting off the chill!

THE CAKE

A friend of the bride and groom who, although a professional pastry chef, had not ever made a wedding cake but created something special for Nina and Daniel. No worries here because this bride and groom like things unique! An arrangement of several cakes on pedestals had a friendly homey feeling that was just what they wanted. The cake insured there was something for everyone with its chocolate flavor and raspberry filling topped with white frosting, a dark chocolate drip and red roses. Although much of it was enjoyed, they also served it at the brunch the next day.

NINA JOHNSON & DANIEL MILEWSKI

103

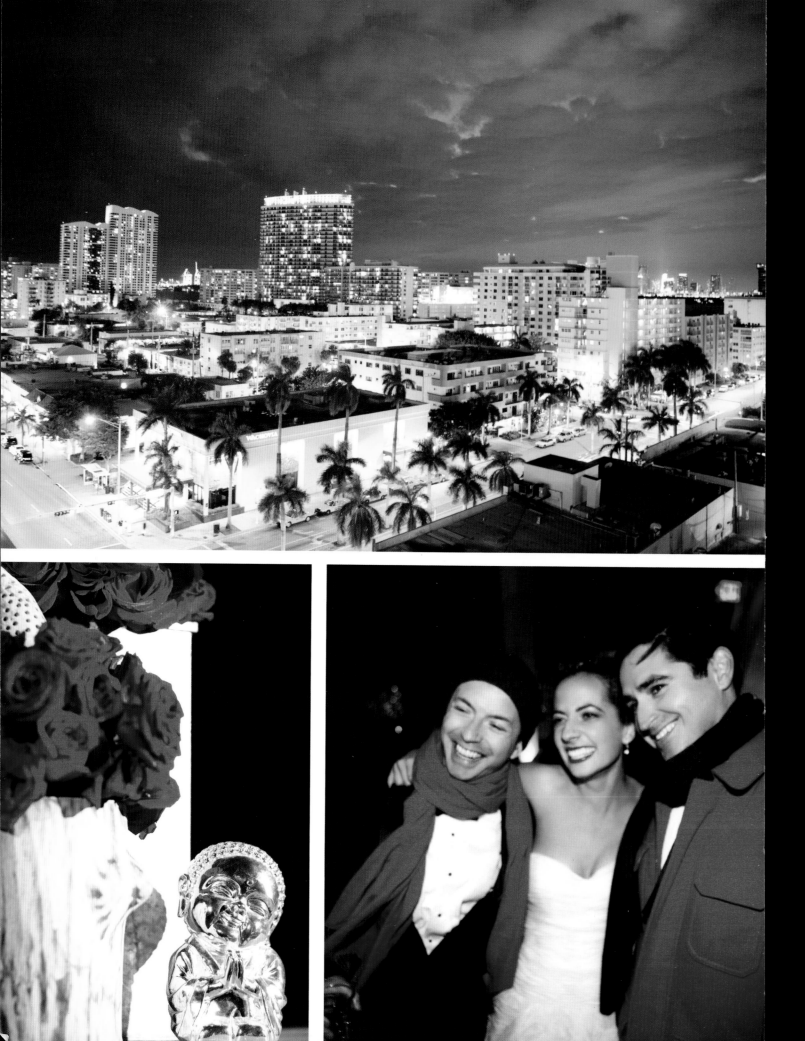

✦ Look for an unusual and unique space for your wedding day celebrations that reflects your interests.

✦ Set a dress code that reflects they way you want your décor. In this case, Nina and Daniel added refinement to their rough space by asking their guests to dress in black tie.

✦ Consider setting up long rectangular tables and serving your food family style for a more intimate and out-of-the-box experience.

✦ For an intimate and meaningful touch, ask family and friends to play a role in the ceremony and reception. They could read a poem, play a song, design the invitation or read a letter.

✦ Nina's Advice for Future Brides: "I would have eaten more! In what could have been an absolutely disastrous situation, we made the most of it. Enjoy it, no matter what, and have a good time."

Lucky Tradition

Something Old: Nina was named after her grandmother who got married wearing a wedding gift from her grandfather, a diamond cross necklace. Nina keeps a photograph of her grandmother on her wedding day on her desk and, of course, wore the cherished keepsake on her wedding day.

Something New: Everything else for the wedding was new!

Something Borrowed: Nina borrowed a beautiful bracelet.

Something Blue: The soles of Nina's shoes were blue.

Loryn Schwade & Nader Panahpour

Loryn and Nader describe themselves as a blank slate when it came to their wedding. From the moment they were introduced through mutual friends, they knew they were in love and continued in loving bliss throughout the planning stages for their wedding four years later. She is a bohemian beauty whose mother is a former interior designer known around Miami for her impeccable taste and sense of style. He is from London and knew his Persian heritage would be celebrated on the first night of their weekend celebration. Friday night's Persian wedding ceremony also served as the rehearsal dinner for the next day's wedding ceremony.

Loryn, a psychotherapist, worked closely with her mother to create a wedding ceremony that was all about love. The black, white and gray event at the Mandarin Oriental Hotel was not what Loren originally had in mind. After Nader proposed to Loren at Fisher Island, the couple had hopes that they could marry there but, as the guest list grew, they realized that they would need a larger space. Plan B was just as gorgeous and they were able to accommodate all of their friends and family.

THE GOWN

Loryn and her mother selected a gorgeous gown by Vera Wang but Loryn didn't stop there. Her accessories complemented her everyday style, laid back but beautiful. She wore a long chain of diamonds by the yard down her back instead of the front! She also wore flowers in her hair but instead of pinning one large flower behind her ear, many small flowers were pinned throughout.

THE INVITATIONS

Loryn wanted unique but traditional invitations for her wedding. It is a challenge to take a long-standing layout and find a different take on it without jeopardizing the traditional elements. She managed to do it by ordering a card that had a traditional invitation on the front and a beautiful detail of a flower in black and white on the back.

THE WEDDING PARTY

There was a bit of a role reversal when it came to the wedding party of the happy couple. Nader's sister served as his attendant and Loryn's two brothers stood with her. Loryn had been a bridesmaid twenty times before so she opted to include only family in her wedding party. Although it was a break from a traditional wedding ceremony, it was a special way to honor the family members in a meaningful way.

THE CEREMONY

Loryn had to compromise when making the plans for her wedding ceremony but the end result was thrilling. She went to her planning meetings with the idea that she would walk down an aisle with a canopy of cherry blossoms. After her team decided that it would ruin the view for her guests, plan B was once again put into place. Loryn walked down an aisle lined in mirrored cube-shaped tables covered in candles. The gorgeous walkway led her to the most beautiful chuppah with cascading falling orchids and flowers. The chuppah was the most beautiful space Loryn says she has ever seen. It was decadent and covered in flowers. She said it "felt like it was raining flowers."

THE RECEPTION

The decadence continued at the reception. The Mandarin Oriental is famous for its spectacular cuisine, and the long caviar ice bar thrilled the guests during cocktail hour.

Loryn described the room as a celebration of her love for Nader but, though it carried through the white, black and gray color scheme, it had a sexier vibe than the ceremony. The lighting was dramatic and Loryn finally got the cherry

LORYN SCHWADE & NADER PANAHPOUR

LORYN SCHWADE & NADER PANAHPOUR

LORYN SCHWADE & NADER PANAHPOUR

LORYN SCHWADE & NADER PANAHPOUR

Natalie Redmond

SMOKED SALMON TIMBALE
AVOCADO AND CRÈME FRAÎCHE

Mr.
Darius Panahizadi

Mr. & Mrs.
Yousef Panahpour

Mr.
Steven

blossoms she had dreamed about incorporated into the décor as branches were cast onto the walls like shadows.

Each chair was decorated with a monogrammed ribbon that intertwined Loryn and Nader's initials. The black-glass accents on the tables added amazing touches of the sexy dramatic look they were after. Orchids were strung and hung from frames to resemble modern lamps and the effect was awe-inspiring.

THE CAKE

The gorgeous chuppah from the ceremony served double duty as it housed the cake during the reception. The gorgeous cake was all white with a gray bow, and it's dramatic frame added to its dramatic effect.

LORYN SCHWADE & NADER PANAHPOUR

✦ Go to your wedding with an open mind and prepare to embrace a plan B. It might end up being even better than your original idea!

✦ Celebrate your family's heritage with a ceremony honoring their traditions and customs.

✦ Use floral elements from your ceremony again during your reception, just as Loryn and Nader's chuppah was later used to frame their cake.

✦ Reconsider the typical setup for your wedding party and ask those closest to you to play a role. Loryn had her brothers stood up for her and Nader asked his sister to be his attendant.

✦ Loryn's Advice for Future Brides: "Be very organized about greeting every guest by dedicating the first two hours of the reception to meeting and greeting and the rest of the night can be all yours! Make an effort to look like yourself." (Loryn felt too "made up" on her wedding day because her makeup was so different than her every day look.)

Lucky Tradition

Something Old: Loryn wore her grandmother's bracelet.

Something New: Loryn wore some of her own new jewelry to complement her wedding gown.

Something Borrowed: She borrowed some of her mother's jewelry for her perfect day.

Something Blue: The bottoms of Loryn's custom Christian Louboutin shoes were blue.

Stephanie Berman & Eric Raphael

Being set up by friends can be one of the most wonderful ways for a singleton to meet someone. It worked out well for Stephanie Berman, a New York–based publicist, and Eric Raphael, a financial advisor! They both lived on 71st Street in New York, but he was on the East side and she was on the West side! Thanks to their gracious friend, they met anyway.

Their passion for New York City and its cool but classic vibe inspired the feel they wanted for their wedding celebration. They selected the Tribeca Rooftop, an amazing event space overlooking the Hudson River, because it combined their passion for downtown cool and uptown classic looks. It is also a minimalist space, so Stephanie was able to put her own spin on it.

The lofty look and New York–inspired space was a beautiful reflection of the city where the couple met. It celebrated the views and vibe this city chic and minimalist couple was after. They mapped out their inspirations early on by looking through images and defining what they liked. Stephanie noticed her eye kept going back to the same look. She knew she wanted her favorite flowers, white peonies and tulips for a clean natural look, and that light would be an important factor.

THE GOWN

When Stephanie's sister got married two years before her, Stephanie started mapping out what her own wedding might be like, right down to the dress! On a trip to Vera Wang's bridal salon with her sister, Stephanie spotted the gown of her dreams. After her own engagement, she went right back and tried it on and she "just knew" it was the one. It fit her minimalist but classic theme and fulfilled the dream she had for her once-in-a-lifetime gown. As the wedding plans moved forward, she built on the simplicity of her dress.

THE INVITATIONS

When classic New York is your wedding theme, the only place to go for invitations is Tiffany & Co. Although Stephanie looked around at almost every option, she ended up sending classic save-the-dates with a silhouette of the New York skyline and beautiful classic wedding invitations from the legendary New York store.

THE WEDDING PARTY

Stephanie's wedding party included her sister as her matron of honor as well as her future sister-in-law and two dear friends. Vera Wang dressed them all as well. Stephanie selected simple black satin strapless gowns that looked amazing on all of them. To add a personal touch, Stephanie gave them each a monogrammed necklace.

The Wedding of

Stephanie and Eric

April 2, 2011

FROM EVERY HUMAN BEING THERE RISES A LIGHT THAT REACHES
STRAIGHT TO HEAVEN, AND WHEN TWO SOULS THAT ARE DESTINED TO
BE TOGETHER FIND EACH OTHER, THEIR STREAMS OF LIGHT FLOW TOGETHER,
AND _____ R LIGHT GOES FORTH FROM THEIR UNITED BEING.
Kahlah

STEPHANIE BERMAN & ERIC RAPHAEL

131

THE CEREMONY

Knowing that light was important and that the couple would need to get creative filling such a large space on a budget, Stephanie turned to her mother, an artist, for advice. Her mother drew out the room and sketched their ideas. They worked together with their wedding planner, Anthony Luscia of Harrington and Luscia Events, and their florist, Atlas Floral, to create a space that felt warm and inviting. Candles did the trick! There were thousands of them lighting the room and leading the bride up the aisle to her groom. The simplicity of Stephanie's wedding gown was echoed in the candles and simple white flowers. She carried an all-white bouquet of peonies, orchids and gardenias in honor of the groom's grandmother.

The bride and groom were married under a simple chuppah of loose fabric draping that was lit from above by candles hanging from the ceiling. The candles reflected through the fabric and the space simply glowed in the light. The candles gave the feeling of a magical moonlight.

THE RECEPTION

The reception area featured alternating tables in different styles. A few of the tables supported large tree lanterns made of cherry blossoms. Others had low modern square arrangements made of four varieties of white flowers and filled with four tall candlesticks.

The guests were seated and served an amazing meal selected carefully and thoughtfully by the bride and groom and her parents. Stephanie "just knew" that she needed to serve the artichoke risotto appetizer instead of a salad the moment she tasted it! The Tribeca Rooftop prepared and served a meal that met the top-notch standards of any of New York City's finest restaurants.

Stephanie saved the information of a band called Creation that she heard at another event years before. She had it in her "if I ever get married" file and she booked them right away. They had all guests on the dance floor having fun!

STEPHANIE BERMAN & ERIC RAPHAEL

STEPHANIE BERMAN & ERIC RAPHAEL

THE FAVORS

In addition to an all-white candy bar, the bride and groom provided bags for each of their out-of-town guests filled with I "Heart" NY products and city maps. Although their theme was New York in an abstract way for the wedding, they gave it a more literal translation with the favor bags!

BE INSPIRED

✦ Set the tone of your wedding theme with the save-the-date cards. Because they wanted a classic wedding invitation, Stephanie and Eric added a silhouette of the New York skyline to their save-the-dates for a playful and enticing element.

✦ Add special significance to your bouquet by honoring your loved ones. Stephanie added gardenias, the groom's grandmother's favorite flowers, to her all-white bouquet in her honor. When I was married, I carried a simple bouquet of lily of the valley, just as my grandmother had done.

✦ Stephanie's Advice for Future Brides: "There is always a way to figure out your vision and work within a budget. Be resourceful and have fun!"

Lucky Tradition

Something Old: Stephanie wore her great aunt's pearl bracelet, which her sister also wore in her wedding.

Something New: Her new wedding dress was a perfect good luck charm.

Something Borrowed: She wore her mother-in-law's diamond earrings.

Something Blue: Stephanie carried a small white linen handkerchief with her new married initials in blue.

STEPHANIE BERMAN & ERIC RAPHAEL

Amelie Huebner & Yannic Seidenberg

When Amelie Huebner moved to Ingolstadt, Germany, to go to university, she didn't intend to meet the man she would marry in her first semester. After meeting, they soon realized that they lived only two blocks from each other. Their romance developed quickly and she gave up her apartment and became Mrs. Yannic Seidenberg after a romantic beach proposal. They now live in Mannheim, Germany, where Yannic plays professional hockey.

Amelie and Yannic love spending time at the beach. They knew they wanted their wedding to be like a vacation with family and friends at a beautiful beachside hotel. They wanted all their guests to be in a perfect vacation mood! They wanted to host a casual beach party that just happened to be a wedding too! They also knew they wanted to commemorate their special day by watching the sunset with a cool ocean breeze and by spending the day outdoors.

Amelie and Yannic were inspired by the summers they had spent on the seaside in Florida. They decided to get married there so that their loved ones and friends could "see the beautiful place, far away from Germany, where the sun is shining all the time."

The Gown

Amelie spotted the gown of her dreams by Pronovias in an online search but learned that it was not available in Germany! While she was visiting her sister-in-law in Boston, she went to a store that sold the brand and inquired about the dress. They did not stock the dress but they were able to order it. Amelie took a leap of faith, just as she had in her quick courtship, and ordered the gown without seeing it or trying it on. After a few nervous months of waiting, she was able to pick up the dress and try it on for the first time only a week before the wedding! She knew it was a perfect fit when she tried it on and her sister-in-law cried. It was like it was made just for her.

The Invitations

A destination wedding requires a lot of advance planning, especially when it comes to communicating travel information! Amelie and Yannic decided to email their friends all the details in lieu of mailing a save-the-date just for the sake of time. They had guests coming from all around the world, so it was important to get the information out in a timely manner.

The invitations were created by Amelie's best friend whose family owns a printing company in Germany. They made a folding card with a cover showing a heart made of mussels in the sand. Inside the card was a photo of the bride and groom's names written in the sand. It was all wrapped with an ivory bow that held a little tag with an image of the couple's feet in the sand! They wanted their guests to get in the mood for the beach vacation.

AMELIE HUEBNER & YANNIC SEIDENBERG

THE WEDDING PARTY

Amelie's wedding party was made up of her sister-in-law, Rebecca, and her best friends, Bianca and Diana. She gifted them with ivory knee-length baby doll dresses from J. Crew to wear at the beach ceremony. Yannic had two best men, and the bride's niece, Story, was the flower girl. She was precious in an ivory ballerina dress.

THE CEREMONY

The ceremony took place on the ocean lawn at the Breakers Hotel in Palm Beach, Florida. The guests were seated on white lawn chairs facing the ocean framed by two huge palm trees. In each of their seats, they found a fan, as the weather was very warm. Amelie came down the candle- and white-rose-petal-lined aisle carrying a simple bouquet of calla lilies.

THE RECEPTION

After the ceremony overlooking the ocean, the bride and groom led the guests to the reception on the roof deck. When the guests arrived at the reception, they were greeted by a big basket full of white flip-flops in all different sizes. It was decorated with a sign: "Just a little treat for your tired little feet." The ladies were thrilled that they could take off their high heels!

There were five round tables and a dance floor, and everything was white and ivory. Pops of a few light pink flowers gave depth to the décor that was meant to simply highlight the amazing view of the ocean. The guests were able to watch the sunset while they were eating their dinner and the dancing went on for the rest of the evening. Amelie loved the look on the dance floor when everyone was dancing in the new white flip-flops!

Amelie Huebner & Yannic Seidenberg

AMELIE HUEBNER & YANNIC SEIDENBERG

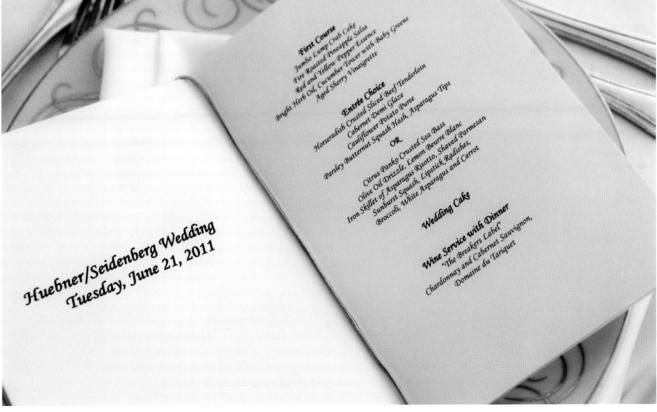

First Course
Jumbo Lump Crab Cake
Fire Roasted Pineapple Salsa
Red and Yellow Pepper Essence
Bright Herb Oil, Cucumber Tower with Baby Greens
Aged Sherry Vinaigrette

Entrée Choice
Horseradish Crusted Sliced Beef Tenderloin
Cabernet Demi Glaze
Cauliflower Potato Puree
Parsley Butternut Squash Hash, Asparagus Tips
OR
Citrus Panko Crusted Sea Bass
Olive Oil Drizzle, Lemon Beurre Blanc
Iron Skillet of Asparagus Risotto, Shaved Parmesan
Sunburst Squash, Lipstick Radishes,
Broccoli, White Asparagus and Carrot

Wedding Cake

Wine Service with Dinner
"The Breakers Label"
Chardonnay and Cabernet Sauvignon,
Domaine du Tariquet

Huebner/Seidenberg Wedding
Tuesday, June 21, 2011

Amelie Huebner & Yannic Seidenberg

151

AMELIE HUEBNER & YANNIC SEIDENBERG

THE CAKE

The bride and groom honored their German roots by serving a typical German cherry-chocolate cake. The cake had four tiers and carried the couple's simple and elegant look throughout, down to the pearl details that matched the pearls on the belt of Amelie's gown.

BE INSPIRED

✦ Consider your wedding celebration a way to share one of your favorite vacation spots with your close friends and family. Amelie and Yannic were able to share Palm Beach, a place they had made special memories at, with their family.

✦ Personalize your bouquet with a special memento. Amelie carried a brooch borrowed from her sister-in-law in her bouquet to add a little sparkle.

✦ Amelie's Advice for Future Brides: "Get a comfortable short dress for the party because it is really hard to dance in a wedding gown!"

Lucky Tradition

Something Old: Amelie wore her grandmother's pearl earrings.

Something New: Amelie's gown was so new that she didn't have an opportunity to try it on until one week before the wedding.

Something Borrowed: A sparkling brooch from her sister-in-law was placed in her bouquet.

Something Blue: Amelie had her toenails painted baby blue.

AMELIE HUEBNER & YANNIC SEIDENBERG

Delia Desai & Patrick Gallo

When music producer Patrick Gallo proposed to Delia Desai, their friends and family knew they would be in for a visual feast when the wedding day came. The bride and groom met on a photo shoot where Delia worked as photo producer and Patrick worked with the artist being photographed. Delia and Patrick set to work on a wedding that would celebrate both her Indian heritage and his love of music. The event that they put together with the help of David Tutera and his team was a true combination of over-the-top Bollywood glamour and a celebratory garden scene from a *Midsummer's Night's Dream*.

Their happy celebration took a lot of careful planning and consideration for the details. New York's Plaza hotel was the perfect location for their happy celebration, and the couple set to work on producing an evening to remember. They looked through photographs of previous weddings and found inspiration in a real Indian wedding that celebrated in bright colors and with true glamour. The groom and the wedding planner really hit it off! This was wonderful for the bride who enjoyed sharing the planning experience with her husband to be.

With their clear vision established, the bride and groom were able to focus quickly on the details for their big day.

The Gown

Delia didn't have that "Aha!" moment that so many brides describe when shopping for their wedding dress. She was about to order a gown that she liked, but her special moment came when she tried on a dress that was not at all what she imagined she would walk down the aisle in. The gown was heavily beaded in embroidery work that reminded her of an Indian sari. That was it! The feeling and moment she had been waiting for came in the gown she least expected it to!

The Invitations

Delia and Patrick went to Ceci New York for their wedding stationery. She gave them proposals that were inspired by Indian textiles, and the bride and groom were amazed. The invitations and paper products for their special day were visually dramatic and would give their guests a true taste of what was in store at the wedding.

The Wedding Party

Delia's six bridesmaids wore eggplant gowns created by Twobirds Bridesmaids. The gowns can be worn in fifteen different ways and each of the ladies selected a different style. It truly is a bridesmaid gown that can be worn again and again! Delia gave each of them a fabulous pair of glamorous shoes to wear, and they all wore layers and layers of Indian bangles that were intended to complement the saris they wore to the rehearsal dinner.

Delia and Patrick's one-year-old daughter, India, also played a special role in the wedding party. With her father, she walked down the aisle in a white dress with a sash that had been embroidered to match her mother's gown.

THE WEDDING OF
DELIA L. DESAI
TO
PATRICK J. GALLO
SATURDAY, THE EIGHTEENTH OF JUNE
TWO THOUSAND AND ELEVEN
AT SEVEN O'CLOCK
THE PLAZA HOTEL

WEDDING CEREMONY

PRELUDE
"All My Life"
WEDDING PARTY PROCESSIONAL
"Viva La Vida"
THE BRIDE AND HER FATHER
"Halo"
HONORING THE MOTHERS
WELCOME AND BLESSING
REMEMBERING VINCENT GALLO
THE BRIDE AND GROOM
Adapted from a Hindu Marriage Poem
THE ASKING
EXCHANGE OF VOWS
EXCHANGE OF RINGS
UNITY CANDLE
"Your Song"
DECLARATION OF MARRIAGE
RECESSIONAL
"Ain't Nothing Like the Real Thing"

THE CEREMONY

The Midsummer's Night's Dream meets Bollywood Glamour theme was evident from the moment the guests arrived at The Plaza Hotel in New York. The ceremony was all white with a soft purple light. The bride and groom wrote their own vows to each other and also lit a unity candle. Delia's cousin read a traditional Hindu love poem in Hindi and in English, and Pat's mother read scripture. During the ceremony, the officiant asked all the guests to hold hands as a symbol of the support system they would be for the new couple. Delia's favorite part of her wedding day was standing at the altar and listening to Patrick's vows.

DELIA DESAI & PATRICK GALLO

DELIA DESAI & PATRICK GALLO

162

THE RECEPTION

The bride and groom wanted the guests to feel like they were entering another world when they walked to the next ballroom for the reception. The white décor faded and was replaced by magentas, purples and, as Delia describes it, "an overdose of bright flowers." There were grand bouquets of flowers mixed with fruits as an ode to the gardens of the Midsummer's Night's Dream. The lights switched from pinks to purples and to reds, which reflected in a henna pattern onto the dance floor in a nod to the Bollywood Glamour they wanted in the room.

In the center of the room was a sweetheart table enveloped under a canopy with two huge chairs. The bride and groom felt like royalty on their thrones while they celebrated. An amazing band played music that had everyone on the dance floor. The band was a last-minute booking after the original plans the couple made for entertainment didn't work out. It ended up being a wonderful result to what seemed like a crisis at the time. The band was followed by a DJ that kept the guests at an after party late into the night.

✦ Define your theme and look for your wedding early in the process. Delia and Patrick found inspiration in two very different ideas but combined them for a unique visual feast of the senses.

✦ Get your groom involved if he wants to be. Patrick was creative and he got along well with the wedding planner. Delia was thrilled when he was able to describe what he wanted in some of the planning meetings.

✦ For a personal touch, write your own vows to each other. If it is important to you, you can take the traditional vows too!

✦ Delia's Advice for Future Brides: "Get a wedding planner you have confidence in. David made our entire process so much fun. Get your hair and make up done professionally."

Lucky Tradition

Something Old: Delia carried a handkerchief of Irish lace from Patrick's mother that she will hand down to her own daughter someday.

Something New: She wore a sari-inspired gown.

Something Borrowed: Delia carried her grandmother's rosary with her bouquet.

Something Blue: Delia's father gave her a ring from H. Stern with a big blue stone.

DELIA DESAI & PATRICK GALLO

Melissa Siebel & Josh Schiller

Melissa Siebel's sisters always look out for her. When her sister Brooke and her husband were on safari in Africa, they met Josh Schiller who was on safari with his family. Instantly they knew he would be great for Melissa and planned to set them up!

Melissa and Josh met in 2006 and, after almost four years of dating, decided to prove that Brooke was right, they were a great match. The couple started making plans to tie the knot at Baker's Bay Golf & Ocean Club, Abaco, the Bahamas. Baker's Bay was the perfect spot because Melissa's family has a home there and it is easy to get to from the East Coast, where many of their guests would be traveling from.

Around 200 friends and family made the trip to celebrate this special couple. The bride and groom wanted a weekend of activities for their visitors, to thank them for making the trip! The warm weather and relaxed environment were the perfect way to celebrate!

THE GOWN

Melissa's younger sister helped her find the perfect Monique Lhuillier gown. Well, almost perfect! The comfortable fit and sweetheart neckline were perfect, but the full skirt was too much for a beach wedding. The tailors set to work on taking out the lining and making a more fitted skirt that was perfect for the relaxed beach setting.

Melissa learned from her sister's wedding days that she should avoid extremely high heels, so she opted instead for a shorter heel that she could stay in all night. The dress changed though! A short white Lanvin number was the perfect dress for dancing the night away.

THE INVITATIONS

A Day In May Design had been a family favorite for a long time, so Melissa turned to them to create a save-the-date with a map of the Bahamas. It is hard to imagine that anyone was able to decline that tempting card! They followed up with an invitation booklet that described each of the weekend events.

THE WEDDING PARTY

It was a family affair from the moment the couple was set up until they started their way down the aisle. Melissa's sisters and her husband's stepsister served as bridesmaids. They selected their own gowns but were guided by the bride. They each wore light tropical shades of pinks, purples and reds. They were the only pop of color in the entire wedding décor scheme!

The groomsmen were the brothers and brothers-in-law of the groom. Melissa's brother-in-law, California's lieutenant governor, Gavin Newsom, performed the wedding ceremony.

MELISSA SIEBEL & JOSH SCHILLER

MELISSA SIEBEL & JOSH SCHILLER

THE RECEPTION

One bay over from the ceremony site, the event team assembled an amazing tent filled with modern décor and a natural vibe. Melissa was very clear in her vision for the tent's décor. She wanted a fun environment that was filled with natural elements. The tent was clear and set with grand rectangular tables to seat guests. Huge phalaenopsis orchids, gardenias and palm leaves were flown in for the arrangements, but the bride insisted that each of the guests was able to see across the table. Simple and elegant white decor with green accents filled the tent.

In the center of the tent was a huge gum elemi tree that the floral team built out so that it looked like it covered and grew over the entire tent. It was built with manzanita branches, and large lanterns were hung throughout.

After the seated dinner and a fantastic round of toasts, the groom surprised the bride with a fantastic fireworks show followed by a junkanoo band that brought drums, music and whistles at midnight. Band members handed out headdresses and got the guests on the dance floor. At midnight, after a fantastic ice cream bar was served, a secret tent door was opened to reveal an after party tent. It had been built out over the ocean on a platform, and a DJ kept the guests dancing through the night.

Melissa Siebel & Josh Schiller

✦ Think outside the box and personalize your wedding. Melissa and Josh collected lots of postcards from the different places they grew up or frequented to use as a guest book. They asked each guest to write a message on a postcard and then the couple put the cards together after the big day.

✦ For a destination wedding, use local traditions to add a new flavor to your celebration as Melissa and Josh did with the junkanoo band.

✦ Melissa's Advice for Future Brides: "Don't worry about all of the little details. Find a few things that really matter to you and concentrate on them."

Lucky Tradition

Something Old: Melissa wore a garter belt that had been passed down.

Something New: She also wore diamond bracelet that was a gift from her husband.

Something Borrowed: The Fred Leighton star earrings she wore in her hair were borrowed from her mother.

Something Blue: The garter belt and a handkerchief she kept in her purse from her grandmother were blue.

MELISSA SIEBEL & JOSH SCHILLER

CONCLUSION

Finding the inspiration for your own big day should be a fun and inspirational process that kicks off your wedding journey. Careful thought and love were put into the weddings featured here. Each of the brides included put a tremendous amount of time, energy and love into creating a look and a mood for their big day based on their own inspirations. I hope you find inspiration all around you for your wedding.

You can find inspiration anywhere, from a walk in the park to a blog! Keep your eyes open to the things that are all around you and collect images that might spark new wedding ideas in you. One of my personal favorite places to find inspiration is in the generations of couples that came before us. Ask your parents and grandparents about their weddings and their heritage. Keep asking them questions or looking at their photographs until you find something that ignites a spark in you.

All the fun design decisions and details for a wedding are a great way to express your personal style as a couple. Get your partner involved in finding inspiration and it will be a memorable and meaningful way for the two of you to contribute to your big day together.

There are so many benefits to clearly defining your wedding style early in the planning process. All of your family, friends and wedding vendors will be able to see your vision and help you bring it to life. Most importantly, it will make every decision you face as a bride, from selecting invitations to choosing ceremony music, much easier.

I hope you find inspiration in the weddings and advice featured here and that you will enjoy your wedding-planning process. Use your engagement as a time to form lasting memories and connections with the ones you love. When you look back and reflect on your own wedding, I hope you smile and see that everything from your wedding décor to your guest list was a reflection of the meaningful things in your lives.

RESOURCES

Laurie Arons Special Events, LLC

1850 Union Street, Studio 2

San Francisco, CA 94123

415.332-0600

www.lauriearons.com

events@lauriearons.com

Camille Styles Events

P.O. Box 302798

Austin, TX 78703

www.camillestyles.com

camille@camillestyles.com

James Farmer Incorporated

103 White Columns Drive

Kathleen, GA 31047

www.allthingsfarmer.com

www.jamesfarmer.com

Tara Guérard Soiree

54 Chapel Street

Charleston, SC 29403

843.577.5006

307 – 7th Avenue, Suite 2308

New York, NY 10001

640.329.6258

Mathes and Co. Events

25 Highland Park Village, No. 100-514

Dallas, Texas 75205

214.350.6360

www.mathesandco.com

mathes@mathesandco.com

Susan Spindler Designs

www.susanspindlerdesigns.blogspot.com

214.405.0118

susanmspindler@gmail.com

todd.event design.creative services

1444 Oak Lawn Avenue, Suite 206

Dallas, TX 75205

214.749.0040

www.toddevents.com

Valley & Co.

Pacific Northwest and
Southern California areas

858.349.9900

206.250.2055

www.valleyandco.com

hello@valleyandco.com

Mary Wright-Shah

Diamond Affairs Weddings &
Events, Inc.

6414 Lakewood Boulevard

Dallas, TX 75214

214.223.8000

www.diamondaffairs.com

Xquisite Events

1141 South Rogers Circle, Suite 2

Boca Raton, FL 33487

561.988.9798

www.xquisiteeventsfl.com

The Zanadu Group

3389 Sheridan Street, No. 15

Hollywood, FL 33021

954.986.9488

www.zanadugroup.com

info@zanadugroup.com